That Woman, Miss Lewinsky

A Play in One Act by

Louis E.V. Nevaer

Based on a true political sex scandal

Publication date: October 2014

ISBN 978-1-939879-17-2

Contact publisher for additional copies and performance
rights information:

>   Hispanic Economics, Inc.
>   P.O. Box 140681
>   Coral Gables, FL 33114-0681
>   *info@hispaniceconomics.com*

>   Cover and interior design by John Clifton
>   *johnclifton.net*

DEDICATION

For Dr. Bernard Lewinsky—and every other father
whose child has been targeted by a predator.

SYNOPSIS

On January 26, 1998, President Bill Clinton tells the American people, "I did not have sexual relations with that woman, Miss Lewinsky." Monica Lewinsky, twenty-one years old when she first arrived at the White House, becomes the center of a political storm. Disclosure of this extramarital affair results in an investigation that leads the U.S. House of Representatives to impeach the president later that year. After a twenty-one day trial by the Senate, Mr. Clinton is acquitted of the charges of perjury and obstruction of justice. This one-act play imagines, from the vantage of hindsight, this unfortunate episode in American presidential history.

CAST OF CHARACTERS

MONICA LEWINSKY, a forty-year-old woman

YOUNG MONICA, a twenty-something White House
staffer

BILL CLINTON, President of the United States

HILLARY CLINTON, his wife

MEDEA OF DESTRUCTION, a sorceress-witch

SETTING

The entire action of the play takes place in the Oval
Office of the White House, Washington D.C.

SYNOPSIS OF SCENES

Scene 1

October 1, 2014

An image of the Hacienda Temozón on the outskirts of Mérida, Mexico, is projected on the stage. A banner in front reads: "Welcome President Al Gore / Bienvenido Presidente Al Gore." A forty-year-old woman, MONICA LEWINSKY, *walks center stage.*

MONICA LEWINSKY. President Al Gore? What? Al Gore has never been president of the United States. Oh, but wait a minute. That banner did exist—even if it was never displayed. To understand why this banner was created in the first place, you have to remember a few things. First, the U.S. holds annual summits with our neighbors. Every year our president travels to Canada to meet with the Canadian prime minister. He also travels to Mexico to confer with the Mexican president. And once each year our president hosts both the Canadian prime minister and the Mexican president. Second, these summits are planned years ahead of time. And third, it turns out that in 1999, when this banner was created, the U.S.–Mexico Summit between Bill Clinton and Mexican president Ernesto Zedillo was scheduled to take place at the Hacienda Temozón near Mérida, a city of almost one million people in Mexico's Yucatán peninsula. That's the Hacienda you see there. And the reason there is a banner welcoming President Al

Gore is that this summit was scheduled to take place less than twenty-four hours after the U.S. Senate would vote to convict or to acquit President Bill Clinton, who was on trial for perjury and obstruction of justice after he was impeached by the U.S. House of Representatives. The Mexican government did not know whether Bill Clinton would be convicted. They only knew that if he was convicted, Al Gore would immediately be sworn in as president—and the first event on his calendar would be to fly to the Yucatán peninsula for the U.S.–Mexico Summit. And so the Mexicans were forced to prepare duplicates of everything: banners welcoming President Bill Clinton and banners welcoming President Al Gore; state dinner menus honoring President Bill Clinton and First Lady Hillary Clinton and state dinner menus honoring President Al Gore and First Lady Tipper Gore. That Bill Clinton was acquitted meant that the Mexicans shredded everything that read "President Al Gore." *(She moves to the banner that reads "Welcome President Al Gore" and removes it, revealing another banner beneath it that reads "Welcome President Bill Clinton." She wipes her hands after she places the banner on the floor.)* I'll bet you never knew Mexico prepared an official presidential welcome for President Al Gore. Here's something else you probably don't know, even if you think you know everything about me, Miss Lewinsky. I am a Latina. My father, Bernard Lewinsky, is from El Salvador. My grandparents Susi and George Lewinsky immigrated to that country in the 1920s. As the

Census Bureau can confirm, I am, on my father's side, a first-generation American, a Latina Jew. But forget the banners welcoming President Al Gore to Mexico and forget the fact that I am the daughter of a Latin American immigrant. *(The image of the Hacienda Temozón disappears and the banner reading "Welcome President Bill Clinton" falls to the ground.)* What I want to tell you is how it came that Bill Clinton found himself in the regrettable position of being the only president of the United States of America who, by court order, had blood drawn to confirm that his DNA stained my blue dress. *(The screen on which the image of the Hacienda Temozón was projected lifts, revealing the Oval Office.* BILL CLINTON *is standing, looking down at his desk. The door is open and in the adjacent room* YOUNG MONICA *is visible.* YOUNG MONICA *is fidgeting, as she peers in, trying to grab a glimpse of the president.)* In the summer of 1995 I was twenty-one years old. I was an unpaid summer intern for Chief of Staff Leon Panetta. See for yourself.

*(*YOUNG MONICA *slowly steps into the doorway and looks at the president.)*

YOUNG MONICA. Mr. President?

(He looks up.)

BILL CLINTON. Yes?

(She walks in, nervously holding files in her hand.)

YOUNG MONICA. I have some papers for you from Mr. Panetta.

BILL CLINTON. From Leon?

YOUNG MONICA. Yes, I'm his summer intern.

BILL CLINTON. Did he send you over?

YOUNG MONICA. I wanted . . . to be helpful. He wants

you to see these papers for your meeting later this afternoon. *(She hands the files to the president.)* Here, Mr. President.

BILL CLINTON. *(With hesitance.)* Yes, thank you. *(Pause.)* Usually, Leon brings these over to me himself, or my secretary, Betty Currie . . . Where? . . . Who allowed you to come in?

YOUNG MONICA. Ms. Currie was busy out there. She didn't notice me. I just slipped in. I hope I haven't done something wrong. I just want to be helpful, Mr. President.

(There is an awkward pause as BILL CLINTON *looks over* YOUNG MONICA. *He smiles. She is somewhat nervous, afraid she did something wrong.)*

BILL CLINTON. What's your name, young lady?

YOUNG MONICA. Monica Lewinsky.

BILL CLINTON. Lewinsky? Is that a Jewish name?

YOUNG MONICA. *(With sincerity.)* It doesn't have to be!

BILL CLINTON. *(He laughs.)* It makes no difference to me, Miss Lewinsky.

YOUNG MONICA. I'm very secular. I don't have any dietary restrictions. I don't even like kosher food—I'll eat anything!

BILL CLINTON. That's good to know.

YOUNG MONICA. I hope all the papers are in order, Mr. President.

BILL CLINTON. *(Looking through the papers.)* Where are you from, Miss Lewinsky?

YOUNG MONICA. California.

BILL CLINTON. Is that right? I love California. As a matter of fact, one of my favorite songs is "California Girls" by the Beach Boys.

YOUNG MONICA. Is it? I've heard of the Beach Boys—but I don't know their music.

BILL CLINTON. *(Surprised.)* You don't? I imagine it's

before your time, a young girl like you. *(Singing softly.)* "Wish they all could be California Girls." That's how it goes. I wanted that to be the convention song next year. But it won't be.

YOUNG MONICA. *(Shaking her head.)* Is that a jingle from a television commercial?

BILL CLINTON. You *are* young, Miss . . .

YOUNG MONICA. Lewinsky. Monica Lewinsky.

BILL CLINTON. Miss Lewinsky.

(He looks at her and there is an awkward moment.)

YOUNG MONICA. "California Girls." I guess I'm a California girl myself, Mr. President. My hometown is San Francisco.

BILL CLINTON. Well, wouldn't you know? You're a California girl—and one without dietary restrictions.

(They pause.)

YOUNG MONICA. So, may I ask, Mr. President, why won't that song be the theme music for the Democratic National Convention? I mean, if you want it to be. You're the president, right?

BILL CLINTON. Hillary. My wife.

YOUNG MONICA. Mrs. Clinton?

BILL CLINTON. She thinks we have to choose a more strategic song. But I don't think that one song will make that much of a difference. That's why I wanted "California Girls." You'd think I'd get what I want. Would make sense, since I'm the president.

YOUNG MONICA. I guess so, Mr. President.

BILL CLINTON. Yes, it does make sense—at least to me, Monica. Do you mind if I call you Monica—it'll be easier for me to remember. *(Flirting.)* The softness of your cheeks and the way your hair frames your face reminds me of the Mona Lisa.

Monica Lewinsky. Mona Lisa.

(YOUNG MONICA blushes and looks down.)

YOUNG MONICA. You are the president, Mr. President.

BILL CLINTON. That's reassuring to know, that I'm the president. Tell that to Hillary. *(He chuckles.)* Now, Monica, I wanted "California Girls" to be the theme song for the reelection campaign, but Hillary is convinced that's a bad choice. She told me that Fleetwood Mac would resonate with the broadest constituency. She pointed out that *Rumors*, their album, was the best-selling record of the entire decade of the seventies. *(He shrugs.)* It's a good strategy, I imagine. The best-selling rock album of the seventies means that any song from that record will make the greatest number of voters nostalgic. She thinks "Don't Stop" is ideal. *(He sings softly.)* "Don't stop thinking about tomorrow." She said it is perfect. *The* perfect choice.

YOUNG MONICA. I never knew that was a real song.

BILL CLINTON. Yes, it's a real song by an old rock group. *(He pauses.)* Hillary, you see, Monica, wants a song that encourages Baby Boomer voters to think about the future with nostalgia. I'm not sure how longing for the past can create excitement for the future.

YOUNG MONICA. I see your point. Unless the future is retro, like looking back at the Capri pants Audrey Hepburn wore and seeing the new Capri pants from the Gap. I love that store.

BILL CLINTON. Well, Monica, the truth is everything Hillary does is calculated. And the truth is Hillary can't stop thinking about tomorrow. But she happens to be right about that song, I have to say. The conventioneers will go wild when that song is played. They'll wave flags. Sing along. "Don't stop thinking about tomorrow." It will be a hit. The thinking about tomorrow part. They will love it.

YOUNG MONICA. And what about you, Mr. President? What can't you stop thinking about?

BILL CLINTON. Me? I'm also always thinking . . . Though right now, well, I can't stop thinking—but it's not *tomorrow* that I can't stop thinking about *right now*, Monica, you "California Girl." *(He smiles as they make eye contact and stare at each other. He sings softly.)* "Don't stop thinking about . . ."

(The Oval Office darkens and MONICA LEWINSKY *addresses the audience.)*

MONICA LEWINSKY. Can you believe it? He spoke to me! He joked with me! He even flirted with me! The president of the United States of America confided to me that he wanted a Beach Boys song played at the Democratic National Convention in 1996 but that Mrs. Clinton vetoed his choice, because she thought that Fleetwood Mac would have greater resonance with a larger number of Baby Boomer voters. I told him that the government shutdown aside, there was going to be a birthday party at Mr. Panetta's office later in the day. I asked if he could stop by. He said he'd think about it. Always thinking. Before I turned around to leave, he told me that I wasn't in trouble, but that I should not walk into the Oval Office the way I had done. Then, as I was leaving, he softly sang words from a song I didn't recognize at the time. The president sang for me. *(She sings softly.)* "All I want is to see you smile, if it takes just a little while."

Scene 2

November 15, 1995

BILL CLINTON *and* YOUNG MONICA *are alone. They are standing in the middle of the room.*

BILL CLINTON. Thank you for leaving the birthday party at Leon's office to accompany me, Monica. *(There is a pause as he looks at and admires her.)* Will you be going back to California for Thanksgiving with your family, or are you going to be my California Girl?

YOUNG MONICA. I'll be whatever you want me to be, Mr. President.

BILL CLINTON. It's Bill.

YOUNG MONICA. I . . . I don't know . . .

BILL CLINTON. Well, I *do* know. Call me Bill, Monica.

YOUNG MONICA. If that's what you want, Mr. President—I mean Bill.

*(*BILL CLINTON *moves closer to* YOUNG MONICA. *She steps back. He continues to move closer to her, until she is backed against the wall.* YOUNG MONICA *becomes nervous as his body begins to press against hers.)*

YOUNG MONICA. Mr. President—Bill—what?

BILL CLINTON. Shhhh. Don't say a word, Monica.

*(*BILL CLINTON *suddenly pushes her against the wall. His left hand grabs her right breast. His right hand slips up her dress toward her groin.* YOUNG MONICA's *arms are spread out against the wall; the palms of her open hands brace the wall. She turns her head as if to say no.)*

YOUNG MONICA. *(She protests.)* Mr. President . . .

BILL CLINTON. Shhhh, beautiful Monica.

(The action freezes with BILL CLINTON's *left hand on her right breast, his right hand up her skirt, and his body pressed against hers. A light falls on* MONICA LEWINSKY, *who speaks to the audience.)*

MONICA LEWINSKY. Women are subjected to sexual assault in the workplace every day in the United States. Under federal law, what you are seeing right there constitutes a workplace sexual assault. At that exact moment the Oval Office became a hostile work environment. Bill Clinton was a sexual predator using the power of his position to exploit what he believed was a young, voiceless subordinate. I didn't know it at the time, but Kathleen Willey had accused Bill Clinton of sexually assaulting her in the Oval Office in the same way. If I were your twenty-one-year-old daughter, what would you want me to do? To scream? To kick him in the groin? What would Bill Clinton tell his daughter, Chelsea, to do if she ever found herself in this situation? But on November 15, 1995, alone with him, I didn't know what was coming next. Was I in danger? Was he going to push me to the ground and rape me? I knew other women had accused him of rape in years past. I just knew that my heart was racing, that he was squeezing my breast with one hand, and with the fingers of his other hand, he was feeling my clitoris. This would have definitely been a workplace sexual assault . . . but for one fact: *I wanted him.* And so . . .

(The action resumes. YOUNG MONICA *slowly moves her hands from the wall. She raises her hands to* BILL CLINTON's *head. She quickly grabs his head*

and brings his face closer to her. She kisses him on the mouth. BILL CLINTON, *surprised, jumps back.)*

BILL CLINTON. *(Startled.)* What? What?

YOUNG MONICA. Don't say a word, Bill. I want you too!

BILL CLINTON. No! This is wrong—we can't! . . . We can't do this. It never should have happened. This never happened, Monica.

YOUNG MONICA. But it did, it did happen, Bill. And we know we want each other.

BILL CLINTON. *(In a stern voice.)* This cannot . . .

*(*BILL CLINTON *moves his hands toward* YOUNG MONICA, *as if he is going to push her gently away, but then he grabs her by the shoulders and pulls her to him, embracing her. In a moment, they kiss. The lights dim on the Oval Office. A spotlight illuminates* MONICA LEWINSKY.)*

MONICA LEWINSKY. The fact that I kissed him, under the law, changed everything. This was no longer a sexual assault; I had consented. It was no longer sexual harassment or a hostile work environment because I wanted him as much as he wanted me. Yes, it is true Bill Clinton took advantage of me, but I will always remain firm on this point: it was a consensual relationship. He wanted me as much as I wanted him.

Scene 3

A few days later

HILLARY CLINTON *is alone, sitting at the president's desk. She is going through a stack of files. After a moment,* BILL CLINTON *enters, startling his wife.*

HILLARY CLINTON. Oh, Bill, you surprised me.

BILL CLINTON. I didn't mean to startle you, Hillary. *(Pause.)* I can see you belong right behind that desk. It suits you well.

HILLARY CLINTON. Why not?

BILL CLINTON. But for now, it's *my* desk.

(HILLARY CLINTON *stands up and* BILL CLINTON *takes his seat as she walks to the center of the office and turns to face him.)*

HILLARY CLINTON. Bill, I don't remember when you bought that tie I saw on the nightstand.

BILL CLINTON. Tie?

HILLARY CLINTON. Yes, that tie. The one that appeared suddenly out of nowhere.

BILL CLINTON. *(Lying.)* I don't remember a tie. You know folks are always giving me things.

HILLARY CLINTON. Yes, but you almost never take anything visitors give you to the residence.

BILL CLINTON. Hillary, it's just a tie. I don't know who gave it to me, or why I took it upstairs. *(She looks at him with a stern expression. He looks over his reading glasses.)* Is that all? A tie?

HILLARY CLINTON. *(Pause.)* No. There's something else.

BILL CLINTON. *(Testy.)* There always is, isn't there?

HILLARY CLINTON. What's that supposed to mean?

BILL CLINTON. Nothing, just that you are always

thinking about something, like a tireless policy wonk. *(He softens.)* But you're my little policy wonk.

HILLARY CLINTON. Save it for someone who gives a fuck, Bill.

BILL CLINTON. *(Taken aback.)* What's the matter with you, Hillary?

HILLARY CLINTON. Who is that young woman?

BILL CLINTON. Who are you talking about?

HILLARY CLINTON. Don't play dumb with me. There's a long history of your screwing around. I know when you're hiding something.

BILL CLINTON. Hillary, you're being ridiculous!

HILLARY CLINTON. All I know is that young woman in Leon Panetta's office has been seen with you on several occasions, and I've been told certain things about her.

BILL CLINTON. What are you talking about?

HILLARY CLINTON. Bill Clinton, I happen to know that at Leon's office birthday party last week a young intern lifted her jacket and showed the straps of her thong underwear to several people. You among them. I also know that you have met with her privately on more than one occasion.

BILL CLINTON. *(Laughing.)* Is this what you're riled up about? Are you jealous of a staffer young enough to be our daughter? Hillary, she's a staff member, just one of the eager young people who is starting out her career in government service.

HILLARY CLINTON. *(Skeptical.)* Are you sure that's all there is to it?

BILL CLINTON. Of course that's all there is to it. I don't even remember her name. All I remember is that she has a gregarious personality.

HILLARY CLINTON. *(Unconvinced.)* Are you sure? I know
    you, Bill.

BILL CLINTON. Hillary, come here. *(She approaches.)* I
    have to say I like it that you're jealous. Makes
    me feel special. But in this case, you're being
    both jealous and ridiculous. I don't even
    remember her name.

*(The lights dim on the Oval Office, and a light
illuminates* MONICA LEWINSKY. *She addresses
the audience.)*

MONICA LEWINSKI. Could she have known this early on?
    That conversation took place Thanksgiving
    week 1995. I was scheduled to start my paying
    job at the White House the following Monday,
    November 26. But already, we had had several
    sexual encounters. The most brazen was on
    November 15, when, after I showed the straps
    of my thong underwear, the president invited
    me to his private study, where we kissed. Later
    that same evening, we had a more assertive, yet
    intimate and consensual, encounter—which was
    interrupted by a call from a congressman. The
    same thing—the interruption of a phone call—
    happened two days later when we were having
    sex. And the tie Hillary argued over was the one
    I gave the president on November 20, hoping he
    would wear it on Thanksgiving Day to remind
    him of me.

Scene 4

Throughout 2009

BILL CLINTON *and* HILLARY CLINTON *face the audience. The room is dimly lit. A light shines on* BILL CLINTON, *who addresses the audience.*

BILL CLINTON. Was it wrong of me? Yes, it was. In the span of five days I had three sexual encounters with Monica and accepted a gift from her. What was I thinking? The truth is I wasn't thinking. I was reacting to events in my life, public and personal. I cracked, I just cracked. That's all there is to it. Why did I crack? I was beleaguered. My mother had died in January. Two months before her passing, the Democrats lost the November elections. I felt unappreciated by Hillary. And then, out of nowhere, this young woman arrived at the White House. She was infatuated with me. She made me feel special— and desirable in the way men want to be wanted. It was a terrible error on my part, no doubt. And I know that when men have unresolved anger, it makes them do irrational, destructive things. Middle age sucks. It just arrives one day without warning. Things hurt, your body is no longer the same, and you see yourself beginning the process of becoming . . . old. My relationship with Hillary had grown distant—certainly the physical part of our marriage. When was the last time I had sex with her? I don't even want to remember. Yes, this may have been a sexless marriage, but that wasn't going to prevent me from having sex. And here was this young woman, who looked at me adoringly. She adored me, and I adored her for that.

(The light dims on BILL CLINTON *and brightens on* HILLARY CLINTON, *who now addresses the audience.)*

HILLARY CLINTON. Our story is part of the human condition, a familiar chapter in the narrative that informs every marriage. I don't care who you are, what society you live in, or the century in question. If you're a human being and you're married, infidelity comes with the territory. I have to be realistic about the way things are in the institution of marriage. Time itself is the enemy. The decades don't pass in vain. Gravity is every woman's foe. What was once perky in our twenties, sags as we approach our fifties. The truth is that women confront a challenge few are prepared to face as we age: hating our bodies even more than we already do. We gain weight around our hips, lines form on our faces, our breasts become an encumbrance. We feel anything but sexually appealing. The truth is that because I felt unattractive, on some level, I was happy that Bill was getting his rocks off— and not bothering me with his tedious, messy sexual urges. Besides, the last thing I wanted was to sense his disgust at the sight of my aging naked body. But I'm not here to beat up on myself. I understand that men, as they enter middle age, also suffer. Their testosterone levels decline. This leads to depression, a loss of appetite for life, and is an affront to their self-esteem. They feel less vital to the world—and less virile. But chemistry is different for men. When a middle-aged man meets a new woman his testosterone levels surge through his body. He feels young and alive. In fact, these hormonal fluctuations are so pronounced that many men confuse the increased blood testosterone levels associated with a fling with true "love." Was Bill in love with Monica? Of course not. But he didn't know it; he confused the exhilarating spikes in his hormonal levels after their pathetic sexual encounters with love. It's understandable. But that doesn't mean I still didn't want to smack the living shit out of that lying, cheating son of a bitch!

(The lights dim on the Oval Office. A spotlight illuminates Monica Lewinsky.)

Monica Lewinsky. She knew. She wasn't stupid. She asked him who I was and why I was in the Oval Office as often as I was. Betty Currie, his secretary, naturally, was uncomfortable knowing as much as she did. She was in a compromised and compromising position. I felt sorry for her, but there was nothing I could do about it. There was nothing anyone could do about it because there was nothing anyone could do to stop the course of . . . *love.*

18

Scene 5

November 13, 1997

MONICA LEWINSKY *faces the audience. The lights slowly rise on the Oval Office.* YOUNG MONICA *is seen pacing back and forth as* MONICA LEWINSKY *speaks.*

MONICA LEWINSKY: You only know about our sexual encounters in the terse descriptions disclosed in the Starr Report. This is what Kenneth Starr wrote of the events of November 13, 1997, when Mexican president Ernesto Zedillo and his wife, Nilda, were guests at the White House. *(She picks up a report from the desk and reads.)* "The following morning, November 13, Ms. Lewinsky tried to arrange a visit with the president. She called repeatedly but suspected that Ms. Currie was not telling the president of her calls. Around noon, Ms. Currie told Ms. Lewinsky that the president had left to play golf. Ms. Lewinsky, in her own words, "went ballistic." After the president returned from the Army-Navy Golf Course in the late afternoon, Ms. Lewinsky told Ms. Currie that she was coming to the White House to give him some gifts. Ms. Currie suggested that Ms. Lewinsky wait in Ms. Currie's car in the White House parking lot. Ms. Lewinsky went to the White House only to find that the doors to Ms. Currie's car were locked. Ms. Lewinsky waited in the rain. Ms. Currie eventually met her in the parking lot, and, in Ms. Lewinsky's words, they made a "bee-line" into the White House, sneaking up the back stairs to avoid other White House employees, particularly presidential aide Stephen Goodin. Ms. Lewinsky left two small gifts for the president with Ms. Currie, then waited alone for about half an hour in the Oval Office study. In the study, Ms. Lewinsky saw several gifts she had given the president, including *Oy Vey! The Things They Say: A Guide to Jewish Wit*, Nicholson Baker's novel *Vox*, and a letter opener decorated with a frog. The president finally joined Ms. Lewinsky in the study, where they were alone for only a minute or two. Ms. Lewinsky gave him an antique paperweight in the shape of the White House. She also showed him an email describing the effect of chewing Altoids mints before performing oral sex. Ms. Lewinsky was chewing Altoids at the time, but the president replied that he did not have enough time for oral sex. They kissed, and the president rushed off for a state dinner with president Zedillo." *(She looks up and addresses the audience.)* That's what the Starr Report says because that's what I told the investigators. But do you think I waited in the Oval Office study for half an hour? Hardly. You know how uncomfortable that study is—cramped and stuffy. Let me assure you that things went *down* quite differently. . . . See for yourself.

(The spotlight dims on MONICA LEWINSKY *and the Oval Office is now fully lit.* YOUNG MONICA *is fidgeting, glancing at her watch as she paces. The door opens and* BILL CLINTON *enters.)*

BILL CLINTON. Today's a bad day—I'm sorry I've kept you waiting, Monica.

YOUNG MONICA. You went to play golf? You actually

stood me up for a game of golf?

BILL CLINTON. I do have obligations, Monica. Look at
me, dressed up. *(He moves his hands, showing
off his dinner jacket.)* There's a state dinner for
the Mexican president. I can't be late for that.
Do you forgive me?

YOUNG MONICA. *(She looks at* BILL CLINTON *and
smiles.)* You know I can't stay mad at you, Bill.
Although I do have the right to be angry. But I
forgive you, especially when you look so
handsome.

BILL CLINTON. And look at you. With your hair damp,
you look like a little wet mouse.

YOUNG MONICA. It's that stupid Betty Currie. She
didn't leave her car unlocked like she said she
would. I stood there in the rain for a few
minutes like an idiot!

(He moves closer to her.)

BILL CLINTON. Come here, sweetheart, I'll dry you off.

YOUNG MONICA. *(Approaching him.)* I have a present
for you.

BILL CLINTON. Why do you spend your money on me?

YOUNG MONICA. Because it makes me happy, silly boy!

*(*YOUNG MONICA *picks up her bag, opens it, and hands
him a small box.* BILL CLINTON *opens it and
takes out the paperweight in the shape of the
White House.)*

BILL CLINTON. Come here, you.

(She moves to him.)

YOUNG MONICA. Do you like it?

BILL CLINTON. Of course I do. I like everything about
you, my Mona Lisa!

*(He kisses her. He puts the paperweight down and
YOUNG MONICA reaches for her purse again,*

taking out a canister of Altoids.)

YOUNG MONICA. Here, take some mints.

BILL CLINTON. Altoids?

*(*BILL CLINTON *takes a couple of Altoids and puts them in his mouth.)*

YOUNG MONICA. Yes, I have that email with me that explains how great oral sex is with Altoids—a tingling sensation that's cool and crisp.

BILL CLINTON. Cool and crisp from someone with hot lips and a luscious tongue?

YOUNG MONICA. We're about to find out.

BILL CLINTON. *(Shakes his head.)* No time. State dinner in a few minutes—I can't be late, Monica.

YOUNG MONICA. Come on, Bill. I'm here. *We're* here. You know you want me.

BILL CLINTON. No, no, no.

*(*YOUNG MONICA *takes* BILL CLINTON *by the hand and they move to the sofa. She reclines and he leans toward her, kissing her on the neck.)*

YOUNG MONICA. Blow gently. I want to feel the Altoids tingle my skin, Bill.

*(*BILL CLINTON *blows gently as he kisses her neck. He helps her remove her dress, revealing her silk slip. He caresses her breasts, cupping one with his left hand while his right hand supports the back of the sofa.* YOUNG MONICA *moans softly with approval.)*

BILL CLINTON. How does it feel?

YOUNG MONICA. It feels wonderful.

*(*BILL CLINTON, *emboldened, pulls off her slip, exposing her bra and naked midriff. He slowly moves down her body, kissing her breasts and resting his head on her abdomen.* YOUNG MONICA *arches her back as* BILL CLINTON *moves farther down to her groin, his face on her panties as he*

unzips his trousers.)

BILL CLINTON. Do you like it, my lovely girl?

YOUNG MONICA. Yes, yes, I do. I love it, my baby boy. I want to feel your breath between my legs. Take my panties off, Bill. I want you to breathe on me right there . . .

(He begins to remove her panties. Suddenly there is a pounding on the door to the Oval Office. HILLARY CLINTON's voice is heard.)

HILLARY CLINTON. *(In a loud voice.)* Bill! We're late!

(Startled, BILL CLINTON pulls away from YOUNG MONICA. He stands, zips his trousers, and straightens his jacket. YOUNG MONICA also stands, puts on her slip, and puts on her blue dress, moving her hand through her hair as she straightens up.)

BILL CLINTON. Hillary, what's up?

HILLARY CLINTON. *(Angry.)* What the fuck do you mean, what's up? What are you doing? We have a dining room full of spics—and you're late? The sooner dinner's over, the sooner we'll get them out. Bill, do you hear me? What are you doing in there?

(BILL CLINTON motions to YOUNG MONICA, pointing to the door leading to the study. YOUNG MONICA, without saying a word, nods her head. She exits the Oval Office. BILL CLINTON hurries to the door as HILLARY CLINTON resumes her pounding.)

HILLARY CLINTON. *(Enraged.)* Bill Clinton! Open this fucking door right now—or I'll have the Secret Service kick it in!

BILL CLINTON. *(Opening the door.)* All right already!

HILLARY CLINTON. *(Enraged.)* What were you doing?

(With suspicion.) Were you alone?

BILL CLINTON. Of course I'm alone. I was on a call with Boris Yeltsin.

HILLARY CLINTON. Boris Yeltsin? You're so full of shit!

BILL CLINTON. We'll talk about this later.

(HILLARY CLINTON resists. She walks into the center of the office, moving her head the way reptiles do when detecting a scent.)

HILLARY CLINTON. Alone? I don't believe you.

BILL CLINTON. Yes, I was alone.

(He reaches for her elbow, but she pulls back. They stare at each other intently. HILLARY CLINTON then moves close to him, sniffing his neck and collar.)

HILLARY CLINTON. Perfume? I smell a woman's perfume.

BILL CLINTON. You're imagining things! It's Altoids.

(He opens his mouth to show her the crushed mints on his tongue. HILLARY CLINTON stands back and looks at him, moving her eyes up and down. She pauses. Then, with her right hand, she reaches and squeezes his crotch. She feels his tumescent penis. Immediately, she lets go of him and stands back.)

HILLARY CLINTON. *(Enraged.)* You lying . . . adulterous . . . son of a bitch!

(HILLARY CLINTON slaps BILL CLINTON across the face. He recoils.)

BILL CLINTON. Hillary, it's not what you think!

(She turns and walks to the door.)

HILLARY CLINTON. *(In a sangfroid manner.)* Our dinner guests are waiting for us.

(The lights dim on the Oval Office and a spotlight illuminates MONICA LEWINSKY. She speaks to the audience.)

MONICA LEWINSKY. The moment Hillary Clinton felt

his semierect penis, she knew something was up. I was in the Oval Office study. I heard everything. And if you look at the photographs of that state dinner, the word "Guilty" might as well have been stamped on Bill Clinton's forehead. It was evident to the officials, diplomats, dignitaries, and guests present that night. It didn't occur to Kenneth Starr that he should have interviewed Mexico's First Lady, Nilda Patricia Velasco de Zedillo, who was a witness to the Clintons' behavior that evening. Women have an intuition about these things. Had Kenneth Starr interviewed her, he would have learned that Mrs. Zedillo noticed the odd way Bill and Hillary were acting and that she later confided to one of her aides a sentence that summed it all up: *Ese matrimonio no es sano.* That's Spanish for "That marriage is unhealthy." That says it all, doesn't it? But what happened next was something that no one—at least not I—could ever have anticipated.

Scene 6

A few weeks later

Monica Lewinsky *faces the audience. The lights suddenly come up on the Oval Office.* Hillary Clinton *stands in the middle of the office, facing the audience.*

Monica Lewinsky. Over the decades critics and detractors have attacked Hillary. She's been called a witch. A bitch. Frigid. Lesbian. Most of these attacks have been made by men, and there is an undeniable element of sexism and misogyny that motivates them to lash out. But what she did weeks after that state dinner made me realize that Hillary—at the very least—must be a Wiccan! With my own ears I heard her cast a spell to conjure a fiend!

(Hillary Clinton *begins to move her hands in a circular motion, almost as if an invisible crystal ball were suspended in front of her. The spotlight dims on* Monica Lewinsky *as we hear* Hillary Clinton *speak.)*

Hillary Clinton. *(In a slow and deliberate manner.)*
I seek revenge on this black day.
My husband's troubles shall go away.
A curse, a spell, a demonic hex!
To avenge his resorting to tawdry sex!
No blow jobs will he ever enjoy,
For That Woman, now, I shall destroy!

(We hear Monica Lewinsky *address the audience. As she speaks, a figure emerges from the shadows. It is a woman, dressed in robes of various hues of gray, with a pale complexion. She wears a fiery*

shade of lipstick and her hair—orange-red—
stands, teased. She faces HILLARY CLINTON.)

MONICA LEWINSKY. Of course you're going to accuse me
of asking you to suspend disbelief, or that I'm
availing myself to the magic realism of Latin
American literature, but Washington is a place
of magical thinking. That includes witchcraft! It
was as if Hillary conjured a fiend to destroy me
through an incantation! That said, I saw the
creature with my own eyes! Hillary summoned
Medea of Destruction, a sorceress-witch, to do
her bidding. She must have known that this
creature would turn on her, but Hillary's anger
was such that she didn't care. Medea of
Destruction came to life.

(We hear MEDEA OF DESTRUCTION, *who is physically*
without sight, speak to HILLARY CLINTON.)

MEDEA OF DESTRUCTION. Oh, Mistress of mine! I am
at your command!

HILLARY CLINTON. *(In a terse manner, addressing her*
malevolent companion.) Of course you'll do my
bidding. I want you to destroy That Woman. I
want you to help spread lies about her. I
summoned you to help me convince the world
that Monica Lewinsky is a nut and a slut. She's
a Jewish whore. A Latina slut. She's a stalker, a
predator, a threat to the president of the United
States. Hers are the Loins of Perdition! She's a
delusional young woman who believes that all
the stupid fantasies she made up in her head
are actually true!

MEDEA OF DESTRUCTION. Yes, I see. Bill Clinton is the
victim of a ditsy, predatory White House intern!

HILLARY CLINTON. Excellent!

MEDEA OF DESTRUCTION. The girl who was too tubby

to be in the high school "in" crowd is now stalking the president!

HILLARY CLINTON. Yes!

MEDEA OF DESTRUCTION. Like the Glenn Close character in *Fatal Attraction,* Monica Lewinsky issued a chilling ultimatum to the man who jilted her: I will not be ignored.

HILLARY CLINTON. Perfect!

MEDEA OF DESTRUCTION. Ms. Lewinsky must die so that the women of America can have better child care, longer maternity stays, toll-free domestic violence hot lines, and bustling mutual funds.

HILLARY CLINTON. You got it! Now, assassinate her character, my character assassin!

(The lights dim on the Oval Office. A spotlight illuminates MONICA LEWINSKY, *who speaks to the audience.)*

MONICA LEWINSKY. Of course it didn't really happen that way, but when Hillary found out about the affair, you should have heard all the cursing and damning going on at the White House! In my imagination, when she summoned that fiend, it became an unholy alliance between Hillary Clinton and the media she enlisted to attack me. Shortly after Medea of Destruction was summoned, Bill and Hillary launched a public relations offensive. On January 26, 1998, Bill appeared before reporters and denied having had sexual relations with me. See for yourself. *(A video of* BILL CLINTON *stating the following is projected on a screen: "Now, I have to go back to work on my State of the Union speech. And I worked on it until pretty late last night. But I want to say one thing to the*

American people. I want you to listen to me. I'm going to say this again: I did not have sexual relations with that woman, Miss Lewinsky. I never told anybody to lie, not a single time; never. These allegations are false. And I need to go back to work for the American people. Thank you.") Then, to continue their subterfuge, Hillary appeared on the *Today* show on NBC.

(The lights go up on the Oval Office. HILLARY CLINTON *is sitting in a chair. We hear Matt Lauer asking her the following question and then* HILLARY CLINTON *replies. Matt Lauer's voice: "You have said, I understand, to some close friends, that this is the last great battle, and that one side or the other is going down here.")*

HILLARY CLINTON. Well, I don't know if I've been that dramatic. That would sound like a good line from a movie. But I do believe that this is a battle. I mean, look at the very people who are involved in this—they have popped up in other settings. This is—the great story here for anybody willing to find it and write about it and explain it is this vast right-wing conspiracy that has been conspiring against my husband since the day he announced for president.

(The lights dim on the Oval Office and a spotlight illuminates MONICA LEWINSKY. *She speaks.)*

MONICA LEWINSKY. And with that, Bill Clinton, the most powerful man in the world, and his wife set out to destroy me. But not without controversy.

Scene 7

The winter of 1997-1998 and the late summer of 1998

MONICA LEWINSKY *faces the audience. The lights are low except for a single light shining on the center of the Oval Office. Whispers, indistinguishable, are heard throughout. She speaks to the audience.*

MONICA LEWINSKY. The Clinton White House had become a place of lies. On December 17, 1997, the president of the United States called me at home at two AM to tell me that if I was subpoenaed, he wanted me to lie and say that my visits to the Oval Office were to see Betty Currie. Two days later, Bill Clinton lied to Vernon Jordan when he denied ever having had sexual relations with me. On January 5, 1998, Bill Clinton told me to lie about how I obtained my job at the Pentagon. Two days later, I signed an affidavit in which I lied stating that I had never had sex with the president. On January 17, Bill Clinton lied in a deposition in the Paula Jones suit, saying we never had sex. Two days after that, he met with Betty Currie to coordinate the lies in their testimony about the reasons for my White House visits. Hillary Clinton continued to lie to protect their political brand—even after the Drudge Report, in their "world exclusive," mentioned me by name for the first time. Oh, and before you forget, while all this lying was going on in the winter of 1998, the world wasn't standing still. In February 1998—between the meetings Bill Clinton and

Betty Currie had about how to lie to cover up the reasons for my visits to the Oval Office—in Afghanistan, a man by the name of Osama bin Laden announced the creation of the World Islamic Front for Jihad Against Jews and Crusaders. If his name sounds familiar for some reason, it should. *(The lights go up on the Oval Office.* BILL CLINTON *is at his desk, holding the* New York Times *in his hands.* HILLARY CLINTON *is standing next to him. He is upset.)* Back in Washington, D.C., far from the al Qaeda training camps in Afghanistan, the unbearable burden of living in a world of deceit was wearing down on the president. See what happened on the morning of August 23, 1998.

(The spotlight dims on MONICA LEWINSKY. BILL CLINTON *and* HILLARY CLINTON *engage in conversation.)*

BILL CLINTON. Listen to this, Hillary. "Monica will never let him go. She will be center stage for the rest of his Presidency, doing a star turn at Congressional hearings, granting celebrity interviews, signing book and movie deals." *(He puts the newspaper down.)* Can you believe this? Can you believe the editors of the *New York Times* let that Celtic cunt write this trash? This is character assassination. It is just terrible the way the media are trashing that young woman.

HILLARY CLINTON. Well, I think it's great.

BILL CLINTON. How can being vicious give you such satisfaction, Hillary?

HILLARY CLINTON. Because it's about that Jewish whore.

BILL CLINTON. Don't say that.

HILLARY CLINTON. Okay. That Latina slut.

BILL CLINTON. Don't say that, either.

HILLARY CLINTON. Whore. Slut. Why shouldn't I speak honestly?

BILL CLINTON. Well, I think it's despicable the way that Celtic cunt is trashing that young woman.

HILLARY CLINTON. Don't dismiss those astute editorials, Bill! Those columns are nothing less than distinguished commentary!

BILL CLINTON. *(Taking off his reading glasses.)* Now, listen to me. What's wrong with us as a society is that we are becoming more cynical and vitriolic. Imagine if you're in the habit of having a glass of orange juice first thing in the morning. Now, let's say I place a glass on the counter, pour in a teaspoon of vinegar, and then fill the glass with orange juice. If I serve it to you, you may not taste the vinegar. The following day, I pour two teaspoons of vinegar before filling up the glass with orange juice. If I do this progressively, there will come a day when I'm filling the glass with vinegar and only splashing a teaspoon or two of orange juice. Now, if I've done this over a long enough period of time, you may not even realize that you're starting off your day drinking a glass of vinegar with just a splash of orange juice. That's what the *New York Times* has become, Hillary. Americans wake up and start their day with the acidity of that Celtic cunt's vindictiveness—and that's how they go out into the world. With the taste of her nastiness and viciousness in their mouths. And that's terrible.

HILLARY CLINTON. Medea of Destruction may be one fucked-up sorceress to you, Bill, but at this point, what difference does it make? She's doing my bidding, getting back at that cocksucking intern. In fact, I find it delightfully ironic that a Catholic cunt is attacking a Latina slut in the pages of a newspaper published by a Jewish schmuck!

(The lights dim on the Oval Office. A spotlight illuminates MONICA LEWINSKY, *who addresses the audience.)*

MONICA LEWINSKY. I knew Bill still had feelings for me. Because a moment later, when Hillary called me whore again, he turned to her and told her to go fuck herself. When a man tells his wife to go fuck herself, that's evidence that his feelings for his mistress are true. You don't believe me? You want more proof? I'll bet you didn't know that Bill Clinton cast a curse on Medea of Destruction. I'll show you how I imagined it.

(The spotlight dims on MONICA LEWINSKY. *A spotlight illuminates* BILL CLINTON, *who speaks to the audience.)*

BILL CLINTON. Now, I may not be a Wiccan or a warlock, or whatever. But I am capable of making a curse if I want to. And I do want to curse that Celtic cunt. May Medea of Destruction hear my words. *(He moves his hands as if to pantomime a spell.)* "Medea of Destruction: May your eggs remain as if frozen in amber, rendering your womb barren. May natural selection put an end to your genetic line, sparing future generations the venom of your viciousness."

(The spotlight dims on BILL CLINTON. *We hear* MONICA LEWINSKY *speak.)*

MONICA LEWINSKY. Isn't that the sweetest thing you ever heard a man say?

Scene 8

September 11, 1998

MONICA LEWINSKY *faces the audience. A spotlight illuminates her. The light slowly rises on the Oval Office, where we see* YOUNG MONICA *and* BILL CLINTON *standing by his desk.* MONICA LEWINSKY *speaks.*

MONICA LEWINSKY. Even as scandal swirled around us, we found time to revisit the discussions we'd had on previous occasions.

*(*YOUNG MONICA *and* BILL CLINTON *speak.)*

YOUNG MONICA. I don't understand.

BILL CLINTON. What's not to understand? It's the way life is.

YOUNG MONICA. No, I don't understand your passivity. I mean, you're telling me that you love me but that you can't be with me. And you can't be with me because you're "stuck" with Hillary in an unhappy marriage.

BILL CLINTON. That pretty much sums it up.

YOUNG MONICA. But it's love we're talking about! Why should what others think stop you from being happy?

BILL CLINTON. It's not that easy, Monica.

YOUNG MONICA. But it doesn't have to be more difficult than it already is!

BILL CLINTON. Someone once said most men lead lives of quiet desperation. That's true for presidents as well.

YOUNG MONICA. Henry David Thoreau. The exact quotation, Bill, is "The mass of men lead lives of quiet desperation. What is called resignation is confirmed desperation." It's from his 1854 book, *Walden*.

BILL CLINTON. I was right to give you a copy of Walt Whitman's *Leaves of Grass* last year as a belated Valentine's Day present, my Mona Lisa.

YOUNG MONICA. Be serious! Why can't we be honest and declare our love to the world? I mean, now that I've been subpoenaed in the Paula Jones lawsuit, it all might come out.

BILL CLINTON. I certainly hope none of this ever becomes public—and I appreciate your efforts to keep anyone from ever knowing about our relationship.

YOUNG MONICA. Yes, Bill. I'll do anything for you because I love you. Didn't I sign an affidavit saying I never had a sexual relationship with you? I committed perjury for you. And you don't envision the possibility of a future for us. After all the lies I've told for you, that's the thanks I get.

BILL CLINTON. Monica, I'm a married man.

YOUNG MONICA. To a woman you don't love.

BILL CLINTON. Come on, now. Love and marriage have little to do with each other, sweetheart. That's the way of the world.

YOUNG MONICA. That's the way of *your* world, but not mine.

BILL CLINTON. Really?

YOUNG MONICA. Yes, because I have faith. I've been thinking about things.

BILL CLINTON. What things?

YOUNG MONICA. Us.

BILL CLINTON. Us?

YOUNG MONICA. Yes—I know you're unhappy in your marriage. But I am realistic about things. It would be difficult enough for you to get a divorce while in office. And it would be even more difficult for you to marry me while in office. I know it would be naïve of me to think I could be First Lady—so there's no pressure from me on that issue! But remember, you have told me more than once that, in three or four years, you can see yourself divorced from Hillary. I'm holding you to your word, Bill!

BILL CLINTON. *(In an avuncular fashion.)* Monica, you are something special. That's why you're my Mona Lisa. When you're older, you'll understand.

YOUNG MONICA. Understand what?

BILL CLINTON. Understand why I can't divorce Hillary. Not now, not ever.

YOUNG MONICA. *(Hurt.)* But why? You told me you're not in love with her anymore! I know about life! The most important thing in life is love. Love conquers all.

BILL CLINTON. *(Laughs softly.)* Oh, Monica, if it only were so. It isn't.

YOUNG MONICA. *(Protesting.)* But it can, it can be for us! We can make it work.

BILL CLINTON. *(Stroking her hair.)* Listen to you. Monica, look around. The fact alone that I am here with you, now, isn't that a betrayal of the vows I made to Hillary?

YOUNG MONICA. *(Protesting.)* But that's different, Bill. You're not in love with her.

BILL CLINTON. *(Putting his finger over her lips again.)* Loving someone is different from being in love with that person. Yes, I love her—but not the way that you might think. I love her as the mother of Chelsea and as the woman who has been by my side in life's journey. Like I said, when you're older you'll understand.

YOUNG MONICA. *(Protesting.)* What? What will I understand that I don't understand now?

BILL CLINTON. *(In a stern manner.)* You'll understand that as the years go by love transforms into respect and obligation. You may no longer be in love with your spouse, but you respect them and you have obligations to them. I'm not in love with Hillary, that's true. But I respect her for being with me all these years, and I have an obligation to her as we age.

YOUNG MONICA. But that's not right. Why shouldn't you have the right to be in love and to be with the woman you're in love with?

BILL CLINTON. Because . . . because that's not how life works, Monica. That's the reality of *my* life.

(The lights dim on the Oval Office. A spotlight illuminates MONICA LEWINSKY.)

MONICA LEWINSKY. He was right about that. I was being a young girl in love. But what mistress hasn't indulged in the fantasy that he will divorce his wife and marry her? That's not the way the world works, I know. Few married men are prepared to divorce their wives, put their children through that ordeal, and then walk down the aisle with their mistresses. What did I know? I was foolish in the way that young people in love are foolish. I believed him when he told me he would divorce Hillary. I even wrote him a love letter based on the movie *Titanic*. I wanted to be his Kate Winslet and have him be my Leonardo DiCaprio. Vernon Jordan, who took on the unpleasant task of helping me find a job, summed it up when he told me that my problem was that I was a young woman in love. The problem with me, he said, was that I thought Bill and I were like Bogie and Bacall. I had to look that up, and I found out that when Lauren Bacall met and fell in love with Humphrey Bogart, he was in an unhappy marriage. The media did not see us as two people in love, however. From the moment my name was published in the *Washington Post*, it was open season. We—or at least, I—was mocked without mercy. I could never escape the relentless venom the sorceress-witch Hillary had conjured: Medea of Destruction.

(MEDEA OF DESTRUCTION *appears to one side. She speaks.*)

MEDEA OF DESTRUCTION. That Grand Canyon of Need—Bill Clinton—was pursued by a relentless woman clinging to some juvenile belief that the president loved her! That tubby loser—so ugly, so pathetic, so delusional! While she is not a stalker, since Bill Clinton encouraged her interest for quite some time, she is certainly aggressive. Otherwise, as a mere intern, she could not have barged through all the protective layers around the president. A little bit nutty Jew, a little bit slutty Latina! One hundred percent loony! Oh, Monica Screwinsky: Never forget, but I'll get you, my pretty, tubby girl! And that adulterous prick, too!

(MEDEA OF DESTRUCTION *walks back into the shadows. A spotlight illuminates* BILL CLINTON, *who addresses the audience.*)

BILL CLINTON. Sure enough, she was in love with me. Was I in love with her—or did I just love the way she made me feel? Young, virile, wanted. The truth is, she made me feel alive in ways I hadn't felt in decades. Was this a betrayal of my vows to Hillary? Yes, but in my defense I have to say that Hillary wasn't in full compliance of her marital vows to me. No, I'm not talking about all that bullshit talk from Republican assholes who have accused her of being a lesbian, or frigid, or a witch. I'm not talking about what all the Republican haters have said about us. What I am talking about is her failure to be the nurturing and understanding wife she should have been. Yes, our sex life was nonexistent, but that's to be expected of most middle-aged couples. Sex just sucks. And it isn't as if I was the first to man to go find in the office what he wasn't getting at home.

(The spotlight on BILL CLINTON *dims.* MONICA LEWINSKY *is now illuminated, and she addresses the audience.)*

MONICA LEWINSKY. Hillary loved the attacks on me, boasting to her girlfriends that I was being "raped" by the media. Bill was furious. In truth, Medea of Destruction's venom proved to be a source of friction between Hillary and Bill.

(The Oval Office is illuminated and HILLARY CLINTON *and* BILL CLINTON *are seen.* BILL CLINTON *is reading the* New York Times. *He speaks up.)*

BILL CLINTON. That harpy at the *Times*—that Celtic cunt.

HILLARY CLINTON. What of her?

BILL CLINTON. She's your shameless shill.

HILLARY CLINTON. No she's not. She's an insightful commentator whose writings merit a Pulitzer Prize. I won't be happy until Medea of

Destruction wins a Pulitzer, Bill.

BILL CLINTON. Is that so? Is vilifying an innocent young woman and destroying her reputation before the world something you admire?

HILLARY CLINTON. Yes, Bill, I do. I admire any fucking thing that will destroy Monica Lewinsky, that Jewish whore you carried on with!

BILL CLINTON. You're despicable, you know that, Hillary.

HILLARY CLINTON. So what? You're stuck with me—you white-trash loser.

BILL CLINTON. God, I hate you sometimes.

HILLARY CLINTON. "Hate" is a four-letter word. And so is "love."

BILL CLINTON. And to you they're interchangeable?

HILLARY CLINTON. All four letter words are interchangeable, Bill. Love. Hate. Fuck. Piss. Shit. I love to hate you, you fucking shit, so piss off!

BILL CLINTON. You are a vicious, depraved creature, Hillary.

HILLARY CLINTON. Careful now, Bill, because I may be a depraved creature, but I am still the mother of your daughter.

BILL CLINTON. You disgust me. Do you doubt why I found comfort in the sincerity of Monica's affection for me?

HILLARY CLINTON. Sincerity? Since when is our marriage about sincerity? It's a partnership, don't you remember? It's nothing but political expediency.

BILL CLINTON. That's right. You will say or do anything to get ahead. You only believe what this morning's polls tell you is convenient to believe.

HILLARY CLINTON. And that's bad? That's strategy! And I'm nothing if not strategic! Do you think I give a damn about that redheaded witch at the *Times*? A bolt of lightning could strike her dead and I wouldn't give a fuck—as long as she's out there trashing that Latina slut who sucked your cock, I'm rooting for her. *(She picks up the newspaper and reads.)* "It is Ms. Lewinsky who comes across as the red-blooded predator, wailing to her girlfriends that the President wouldn't go all the way."

BILL CLINTON. *(Taking the paper back from her.)* You are a cunt, Hillary.

HILLARY CLINTON. You can go fuck yourself, Bill Clinton. All I know is that this is brilliant! *(Grabbing the newspaper from his hand.)* Listen to this, you selfish prick: "It is Mr. Clinton who behaves more like a teen-age girl trying to protect her virginity." I love it!

Scene 9

Throughout 1998

MONICA LEWINSKY *faces the audience. A spotlight illuminates her. She addresses the audience.*

MONICA LEWINSKY. The media would have you believe that I was at fault, seducing a married man. But the truth is that many people knew about Bill's affection for me—and they were his enablers. Betty Currie would come in on the weekends just to let me into the White House. The Secret Service was aware that I was there for "private" meetings with the president. Secret Service records document that the president would head for the Oval Office within minutes of my arrival, especially on weekends. The notes also report that a few minutes after I left, he would return to the family residence. A few months before the scandal broke, one of the agents recommended that I be banned from the White House. Bill Clinton, however, made it clear that he was free to see whomever he chose. And he chose to see me. *(Suddenly, two spotlights illuminate the Oval Office.* HILLARY CLINTON *and* MEDEA OF DESTRUCTION *are sitting on the president's desk with an open bottle of wine. They are drinking from goblets with gothic designs as they engage in their banter.)* You have probably forgotten how relentless the media were in their attacks on me. The Clintons are masterful when it comes to manipulating the media. After my name was made public, I remember the vicious attacks on me by both the Clintons and the press. Remember the public shaming to which I was subjected?

MEDEA OF DESTRUCTION. Look at her!

HILLARY CLINTON. Nutty, slutty—and tubby!

MEDEA OF DESTRUCTION. Yeah, look at those hips!

HILLARY CLINTON. Look at those fat tits!

MEDEA OF DESTRUCTION. Jewish whore!

HILLARY CLINTON. Latina slut!

MEDEA OF DESTRUCTION. She buys her clothes at the Gap! Cheap Jew!

HILLARY CLINTON. She has to! Fat spic!

(They cackle in unison.)

MEDEA OF DESTRUCTION. Monica, you are forever bathed in an impermissible taint!

HILLARY CLINTON. Your father's a wetback!

(MEDEA OF DESTRUCTION pours more wine for HILLARY CLINTON. They women drink up.)

MEDEA OF DESTRUCTION. Hey, that gives me an idea— a brilliant idea!

HILLARY CLINTON. Yeah? What?

MEDEA OF DESTRUCTION. Why don't you take all those Hasidic Jews in New York, put them on trains to the border, and have them build a wall! Jews are great at building walls!

HILLARY CLINTON. What a great idea! And you know what we'd call it?

MEDEA OF DESTRUCTION. What?

HILLARY CLINTON. The Great Wailing Wall of the Frustrated Immigration! We have enough fucking spics in this country already without having that tubby one going after Bill!

MEDEA OF DESTRUCTION. Throw that Latina slut's father over the wall and watch him pound his head as he wails that he can't get back in!

(They cackle in unison.)

HILLARY CLINTON. *(Catching her breath.)* Do you think that we could really get away with it?

MEDEA OF DESTRUCTION. Why not? Didn't every single Hasidic Jew in New York vote for you when you ran for the Senate?

HILLARY CLINTON. *(Laughing.)* Some voted for me several times!

MEDEA OF DESTRUCTION. God, election fraud is my most cherished American tradition!

(The women laugh. HILLARY CLINTON *pours more wine for* MEDEA OF DESTRUCTION. *They women drink up.)*

HILLARY CLINTON. You know, just because she's Jewish doesn't mean she's going to be the killer of this Clinton's political future!

MEDEA OF DESTRUCTION. And just because she's Latina doesn't mean that tubby thing is a Latina lover!

(They cackle in unison.)

HILLARY CLINTON. Medea of Destruction—you are divine!

MEDEA OF DESTRUCTION. Hillary of Expediency—you are presidential!

HILLARY CLINTON. Do you really think so?

MEDEA OF DESTRUCTION. Yes, I do think so.

HILLARY CLINTON. *(Pause.)* May I?

MEDEA OF DESTRUCTION. May you what?

HILLARY CLINTON. May I kiss your tit?

(They cackle in unison.)

MEDEA OF DESTRUCTION. Only if you chew on some Altoids first!

(They cackle in unison.)

HILLARY CLINTON. You know, we could call her an

ethnic working-class bitch.

MEDEA OF DESTRUCTION. Wait a minute. Aren't we also ethnic working-class bitches? I'm Irish and you're Welsh. We're ethnic white trash!

HILLARY CLINTON. Oh, I guess you're right. But what of it?

(They shrug.)

HILLARY CLINTON and MEDEA OF DESTRUCTION. *(Together.)* Ethnic working-class bitch! Jewish whore! Latina slut! Altoids queen!

(A spotlight illuminates MONICA LEWINSKY. *She addresses the audience.)*

MONICA LEWINSKY. *(With sadness.)* The public shaming to which I was subjected was so cruel that my mother flew from California to move in with me. She was afraid that after my dignity had been taken from me, I might attempt to take my own life. My mother gave me life and my mother saved my life. Even Bill Clinton was astounded at the attacks Hillary orchestrated through the media she manipulated.

(Another spotlight shines in the Oval Office, illuminating BILL CLINTON. *He removes his reading glasses and speaks a single sentence to both* HILLARY CLINTON *and* MEDEA OF DESTRUCTION.*)*

BILL CLINTON. There's nothing more pathetic in this world than cock-starved cunts.

Scene 10

February 14, 1999

MONICA LEWINSKY *faces the audience. A spotlight illuminates her. She speaks.*

MONICA LEWINSKY. I agree with Bill. Not in those same words, but misogynist women are the worst misogynists of all. During this entire time I was also attacked by so-called feminists who were blinded by their political ties to the Clinton administration. They could not see how the attacks on me were also an attack on all women and on the integrity of the principles of feminism.

(We suddenly see MEDEA OF DESTRUCTION *emerge from the shadows. She faces* MONICA LEWINSKY *and speaks.)*

MEDEA OF DESTRUCTION. Middle-aged married man has affair with frisky and adoring young office girl. Man hints to girl he might be single again in three or four years. Man gets bored with girl and dumps her. Girl cries and rants and threatens. Bill Clinton is the victim of a ditsy, predatory White House intern! A Jewish whore! A Latina slut! Altoids queen!

*(*MEDEA OF DESTRUCTION *recedes into darkness.)*

MONICA LEWINSKY. The only comforts I found during those terrible months were in the many gifts that Bill had given me. On occasion, he would send over Betty Currie with a box of gifts. I loved the items he bought for me at The Black Dog Restaurant on Martha's Vineyard. I later found out he bought the exact same things for Chelsea. He told me we were the only two women in his life that he loved without reservation. I asked what he bought Hillary and he said he asked one of the Secret Service agents to go to a utility closet and find a broom. I knew he was joking, but he made his point.

(HILLARY CLINTON *appears when a spotlight shines on her.*)

HILLARY CLINTON. That's very funny. A broomstick for this old witch. That's what I'd expect from someone like that woman, Miss Lewinsky. When you are young it is easy to believe the fantasies in which we all indulge, that our lives—our marriages—will be ideal. Keep that in mind, Miss Lewinsky. Reality, however, has a way of upending those hopes and expectations. And the harsh truth is that reality, which is to say life, is harder on women than it is on men. Bill and I met, we fell in love, and we married. We had a daughter and we pursued our careers. I concentrated on raising Chelsea and my work. But I will be honest—and every woman whose husband has strayed will agree with me—what I found insulting was not that he had other women, but the kinds of women he chose! Oh, yes, I understand his fragile ego—which is natural given his childhood. His mother, Virginia, was a waitress who became a nurse anesthetist. Working- class family. His father, a discharged soldier who served in World War II, was killed in an automobile accident three months before Bill was born. Virginia then married Roger Clinton, Sr., an alcoholic car salesman who slapped her around and was psychologically abusive to Bill—and Roger, Jr., the son Virginia had with her second husband. It doesn't take Freud to see the feelings of inadequacy and self-doubt that have been part of Bill's life. And I have used his tragic childhood to justify, to rationalize, and to excuse his tendency to pick white-trash women for his tawdry affairs. But Monica? An intern? What a fucking asshole! Put yourself in my situation. Someone like Paula Jones I can dismiss as a white-trash bimbo. But when he almost raped—and that's what he almost did in the Oval Office—a young, naïve girl like Monica . . . I had no choice but to forge an unholy alliance with Medea of Destruction to punish Bill by attacking someone for whom he cared deeply. I had no choice but to do everything in my power to destroy that woman, Miss Lewinsky. As for Bill, that rotten son of a bitch? Well, all I can say is he's lucky the Secret Service was around, or I would have performed sex reassignment surgery right there in the White House!

(The lights dim, except for the spotlight on MONICA LEWINSKY. *She speaks.)*

MONICA LEWINSKY. Perhaps Hillary did not notice that when Medea of Destruction vowed to get me, she promised also to attack the Clintons as well. Perhaps Hillary thought she could control Medea of Destruction. But Hillary couldn't control the media. When she realized that, she became more enraged—and demented. Bill and I spoke of how miserable his life was with Hillary—and the freedom I offered. His words would prove to be prophetic.

(Lights illuminate the Oval Office. YOUNG MONICA *and*

Bill Clinton *are alone, speaking to each other.)*

Young Monica. How can you stand to live the rest of your life with her after she has worked to destroy me in this cruel manner? How can you stand to live the rest of your life with a woman you no longer love?

Bill Clinton. When you phrase it that way, it's an unpleasant prospect.

Young Monica. I know. So how can you do it? I mean—

Bill Clinton. Well, if it were up to me, Monica, I'd spend as little time with her as possible. If I had my way, I would love it if she decided to run for office. If she were away in Washington in the Senate or something, then I could carry on with my post-presidential life without having to see her face every day. Heck, in a perfect world, she'd spend the rest of her life taxiing up and down tarmacs at airports around the globe— time zones away from me!

Young Monica. Really? Do you really mean that?

Bill Clinton. The way she has masterminded this smear campaign against you? I want to have as little contact as possible with someone that depraved. And that, I admit, is the truth.

Scene 11

December 5, 2000 and October 1, 2014

MONICA LEWINSKY *faces the audience. A spotlight illuminates her. She addresses the audience.*

MONICA LEWINSKY. The truth? The truth is that Bill Clinton has only recently become acquainted with the truth. And the truth is that it has not been easy for any of us since that scandal. Yes, the Clintons have made a fortune. Shaking down publishers for advances on their books. Addressing organizations prepared to pay hundreds of thousands of dollars to hear either one of them speak about themselves and how America would not exist without their selfless work to keep the world spinning, the tides rolling in, the clouds drifting by.

(A spotlight illuminates HILLARY CLINTON, *who speaks.)*

HILLARY CLINTON. We came out of the White House not only dead broke, but in debt. We had no money when we got there, and we struggled to, you know, piece together the resources for mortgages, for houses, for Chelsea's education. You know, it was not easy.

(The spotlight dims on HILLARY CLINTON.*)*

MONICA LEWINSKY. The president doesn't work for free. Hillary forgets to point out that they were "broke" because of the legal bills she and her husband incurred desperately trying to cover up his affair with me—and the enormous expenditures they made to save their political brand. But, apart from the money, things have not gone well for them in terms of contributing to the world. Bill's foundation is fighting AIDS, and that epidemic continues to ravage the developing world. His efforts have also focused on tsunami victims and the aftermath of Hurricane Katrina. Radioactive fish are swimming in the ocean, posing a threat to us. The Ninth Ward in New Orleans remains abandoned. Hillary, who has had two public positions in the intervening years, has not fared better in terms of achievements. She became a carpetbagger who bamboozled the people of the state of New York into electing her to the Senate. And what did she accomplish for them as senator? Nothing. There was no significant piece of legislation passed to benefit the people of New York. She did vote to authorize the invasion of Iraq—only to excuse her vote years later by saying she was deceived by Colin Powell. The truth is that the only thing she accomplished while at the Senate was to position herself for a presidential run. And she lost. Then she left New Yorkers high and dry when she became secretary of state. In short, she used New York the way all carpetbaggers, past and present, have done. Hillary claims to be proud of her record as Madam Secretary. Do you remember what she said?

(A spotlight illuminates HILLARY CLINTON, *who speaks.)*

HILLARY CLINTON. I think we really restored American leadership in the best sense. That, once again, people began to rely on us as setting the values, setting the standards.

(The spotlight dims on HILLARY CLINTON.)*

MONICA LEWINSKY. This is bullshit. I know it. You

know it. Even the editors at the *New York Times* know it. Our country is less respected and we are now more threatened than before her tenure as secretary of state. The only accomplishment she can call her own is the murder at the hands of terrorists of U.S. ambassador Chris Stevens in Libya. The truth is that Hillary's tenure at the State Department has evaporated into the absence of material achievement of the Obama administration she served. This should not come as a surprise since, as we know about Hillary Rodham Clinton, it's always all about her, her, her. The truth is that even Hillary herself can't think of a single accomplishment she achieved while secretary of state. Take it from the *New York Times*. (*She reads from the newspaper.*) "It was a simple question to someone accustomed to much tougher ones: What was her proudest achievement as secretary of state? But for a moment, Hillary Rodham Clinton, appearing recently before a friendly audience at a women's forum in Manhattan, seemed flustered." That was in April 2014. She's a user and a loser.

(The spotlight illuminates MEDEA OF DESTRUCTION.*)*

MEDEA OF DESTRUCTION. There's something poignant about a forty-year-old frozen like a fly in amber for something reckless she did in her twenties, while the unbreakable Clintons bulldoze ahead! It is like a Golden Oldie tour of a band you didn't want to hear in the first place.

(The spotlight dims on MEDEA OF DESTRUCTION.*)*

MONICA LEWINSKY. When news of my affair with Bill Clinton broke, I was arguably the most humiliated person in the world. Thanks to the

Drudge Report, I was also possibly the first person whose global humiliation was driven by the Internet. For several years I tried my hand in the fashion-accessory business and became involved in various media projects, including an HBO documentary. Then I lay low for the most part. Not lying low had exposed me to criticism for trying to "capitalize" on my "notoriety." Apparently, others talking about me is okay; me speaking out for myself is not. I turned down offers that would have earned me more than ten million dollars, because they didn't feel like the right thing to do. I attempted to move on. I moved to England to study, to challenge myself, to escape scrutiny, and to reimagine my identity. My professors and fellow students at the London School of Economics were wonderful—welcoming and respectful. In 2006, I graduated with a master's in social psychology. I liked to joke that I was trading the blue dress for blue stockings, and the degree provided new scaffolding to hang my life experiences on. It would also prove, so I hoped, to be a gateway to a more normal life.

(A spotlight illuminates BILL CLINTON, *who speaks.)*

BILL CLINTON. Didn't I tell you that it would never work out? That I was stuck with Hillary for the rest of my life? That we had to be realistic about things? But I was also sincere, Monica, when I said that you reminded me of the Mona Lisa. Monica Lewinsky, you'll always be my Mona Lisa.

(A spotlight dims on BILL CLINTON.*)*

MONICA LEWINSKY. Mona Lisa? Yeah, right. Now, I'm not saying we've been in contact with each other since he left office. But I'm not saying that we haven't been in contact, either. But if you think that Bill Clinton was celibate for those four long years Hillary Clinton visited every airport in the world where they were foolish enough to give her plane permission to land and accomplish nothing . . . Well, being nostalgic, like a Golden Oldie tour of how Bill Clinton used to be . . . *(With enthusiasm.)* If only you could have been there, on this occasion or that occasion, when Bill was back at the top of his game! I mean the old Bill, before the open heart surgery, before the weight loss that made his neck look like a turkey's, before the bouts of erectile dysfunction consistent with American men in his condition. There are glimpses there, still, of the old Bill Clinton's political brilliance that America elected to the White House. See for yourself.

(A spotlight illuminates BILL CLINTON *standing in the Oval Office, removing his reading glasses, and he speaks to the audience with confidence.)*

BILL CLINTON. The greatest challenge Hillary faces in 2016 is overcoming the nothingness of the Obama administration. My concern is that everything she has ever done has been because of political calculation. That makes her inauthentic. Political calculation catches up with you at some point. Let me give you a couple of examples. If the majority of the country wants to attack Iraq, she votes to authorize a war of occupation. When the country sours on that policy, then she admits her vote was a mistake. If the country opposes same-sex marriage, then she's for traditional marriage. When the country no longer cares

who marries whom, then she's for same-sex
marriage. See? People forget that her only
principles are to repeat what opinion polls tell
her that people want to hear. Hillary doesn't
have the power that comes from the honesty
and conviction of someone who really believes
the policy positions he or she advances. I'm also
concerned that a generational shift has occurred
in the country. After eight years of Obama's
lack of achievement, I'm afraid the nation won't
be enthusiastic about another Democratic
activist. Hillary—like me—is a Democratic
liberal whose views were shaped as a reaction to
the excesses of Reaganomics. Today's voters
don't remember Reaganomics; it's ancient
history to them. Now, I have to ask myself what
voters want. Certainly not an heir to the
wasteland of the Obama administration. Voters
know the country can't continue to stand still,
accomplishing nothing, going nowhere, year
after year. What voters want is an ideological
reaction to the Great Recession of 2008. It's the
economy, stupid. Voters don't want a post-
Reagan Democratic *activist*. They want a post-
Great Recession Democratic *progressive*. I keep
asking myself if Hillary can be successfully
rebranded and repackaged as a Democratic
progressive—and if voters want an old woman
who has me, this dirty old man America loves,
as baggage! The voters might. And, yes, I know
everyone's talking about how Hillary can't wait
to be the first female president. That's all the
pundits want to talk about, but that's not what
concerns me. In the Clinton household, I'm the
one who can't wait to be back in the White

House. Me. Back in the White House. *(He smiles broadly.)* None of the *obligations* . . . but with all the . . . *privileges.*

(The spotlight dims on BILL CLINTON.*)*

MONICA LEWINSKY. On January 19, 2001, his last full day in office, Bill agreed to have his law license suspended so that prosecutors would not pursue criminal charges that he lied under oath about his relationship with me. The suspension ended January 18, 2006. Hooray! Now, I will let you in on a final secret. The official White House records don't document every visit I made to the Oval Office. Remember that Oval Office study where the Starr Report mistakenly says I waited when Bill and I experimented with Altoids? Well, that was my "usual" spot when there were interruptions. On one of my final visits to the White House, we were in that study when Bill opened the door to the Oval Office. Hillary, unexpectedly, was sitting at Bill's desk! He quickly shut the door, told me to be silent, and then he entered the Oval Office as if nothing was wrong. I put my ear to the door to listen in on them. Can you imagine the adrenaline rushing through his veins—his wife in one room and his mistress in the other? Today, it's funny. But when it was happening, it was terrifying. Oh, and if you're curious about what I heard while in the Oval Office study that day, take a look for yourself.

(The lights illuminate the Oval Office. HILLARY CLINTON *is sitting at the president's desk.* BILL CLINTON *is standing in front of the desk.)*

HILLARY CLINTON. After all the shit I've put up with from you, William Jefferson Clinton! You owe me!

BILL CLINTON. You're right about that, I reckon I owe
you.

HILLARY CLINTON. Fucking damn right you do. You owe
me big time! *(She stands and, jabbing her finger
into the desk, speaks).* In fact, you owe me *this*!

BILL CLINTON. *(Confused.)* This?

HILLARY CLINTON. Yes. *(Jabbing her finger into the
desk).* This!

BILL CLINTON. What "this" are you talking about?

HILLARY CLINTON. *(Jabbing her finger into the desk.)*
This!

BILL CLINTON. The desk?

HILLARY CLINTON. *(Laughs. Then she raises her arms
and opens them wide to indicate the room.)* This
office!

BILL CLINTON. This office?

HILLARY CLINTON. Yes, Bill Clinton. You owe me the
presidency!

BILL CLINTON. Aren't you being a little too ambitious?

HILLARY CLINTON. Goddamn you, Bill! I stood by you,
scandal after scandal, year after year. I smiled
for the cameras when I was publicly humiliated
with the revelations that you were screwing
around with a woman young enough to be our
daughter. And that humiliation was flashed
around the world with Internet speed. And even
after that, I still lied for you. I lied to that
balding creep on the *Today* show, saying it was
a right-wing conspiracy when it wasn't. And I've
stood by your side because I had to—to protect
the viability of our brand. *(She looks at him, as
her arms gesture, indicating the room once
more.)* Don't you get it? It's payback time, Bill.
From now on, it's all about me, me, me.

BILL CLINTON. This office?

HILLARY CLINTON. *This!*

(BILL CLINTON *and* HILLARY CLINTON *continue to argue, gesticulating, but their words are not heard. Their shadows are projected on the Oval Office walls. As the lights dim on them, only their silhouettes are seen as they continue to bicker. They resemble two inmates in the asylum of their own ambition. As the Oval Office becomes completely dark,* MONICA LEWINSKY *is illuminated. She smiles for a while before she speaks.)*

MONICA LEWINSKY. They will continue to bicker as people who loathe each other are destined to bicker. The Clintons are trapped in the lowlife melodrama of a bad *Twilight Zone* episode that takes place in a trailer park in Arkansas disguised as the Oval Office. Mexico's first lady was right on the money about this being an unhealthy relationship, Bill and Hillary, two sick old fucks. As for me, I managed to escape this twisted world of theirs. Now, if you remember, the first time I met Bill—Mr. President to you—he sang that refrain from that song telling me that all he wanted was to see me smile, even if it took just a little while. Well, I've learned that in life things often take longer than you think. It's taken more than a little while. But, despite the wait, I am now in a place in my life from which, having risen above the efforts of Hillary and Bill to destroy me in order to protect their hollow political brand, I can smile. Be happy for me. I want you to be happy for me. I am Monica Lewinsky. I can smile. But *this* woman's smile remains as enigmatic as the Mona Lisa's.

FINAL CURTAIN